FASHION ILLUSTRATION TODAY

NICHOLAS DRAKE

FASHION ILLUSTRATION TODAY

With 214 illustrations, 166 in colour

THAMES AND HUDSON

Dates given in captions refer to the year when illustrations were first published, where this is different from the date given by the artist when signing his work.

On the title page: Paris collections. Bernard Perris, Autumn 1985. Watercolour by Joe Eula for 'Harper's Bazaar'.

This page: Fashion study of a back view, 1984, by Tony Viramontes.

© 1987 Thames and Hudson Ltd, London

Printed and bound in Japan by Dai Nippon

CONTENTS

Left: Promotion for New York's Trump Tower, 1986. Drawing by Tim Sheaffer.

Opposite
Three caricatures by Tim Sheaffer of celebrities from the world of fashion.

SINCE THE BEGINNING of the 1980s there has been an international revival of interest in fashion illustration, not just for its practical function of reportage but also as an art form. The most exciting confirmation of this revival has been the establishment of several European publications which choose to commission artists, rather than photographers, to supply their principal visual matter. Outstanding among these are the French magazine *La Mode en Peinture* and Italian *Vanity*, both of which have become showcases for a host of bright, original and daring new illustrators. Established international publications such as the British and American editions of *Vogue*, the European editions of *Harper's Bazaar*, French *Marie-Claire* and British *Tatler*, although still largely committed to photographs, now regularly allocate more pages to illustrations than at any point since the early 1960s. Not since the heyday of fashion illustration in the early decades of this century have artists been given so much freedom to portray fashion as they wish, to experiment and extend the boundaries of the art – in their styles, the media in which they work, and in their choice of backgrounds and subjects. Unlike photography, illustration does not produce a mechanical, unselective documentation of a subject; its point is not that of total recall but of an individual and refined interpretation. Yet a drawing can be more true than a photograph, for by selectivity and discrimination the artist can lay bare the essential.

Up until the early 1960s fashion publications such as *Vogue* and *Harper's Bazaar* gave equal emphasis to both photographs and drawings; but around 1960 several leading artists died, including Eric and René Bouché of *Vogue*. They had been regular contributors for over twenty years, but no one was asked to replace them. Collectively, the leading fashion magazines undertook a clear change of editorial policy: artists were no longer given consistent support, only sporadic and spontaneous commissions. Photography alone was to record the heroes and heroines of the classless new age of youth culture. Newspapers, however, continued to value artists for their skill as reporters and their ability to work quickly under pressure. Tod Draz worked for *The New York Times*, Joe Eula for the *Herald Tribune* and the London *Sunday Times*, and Kenneth Paul Block and Steven Stipelman for *Women's Wear Daily*.

Throughout the lean years of the 1960s and 1970s only one artist was commissioned by the fashion magazines with any regularity – the Puerto-Rican-born illustrator Antonio Lopez. He arrived on the scene in the early 1960s, bringing the bold techniques, colours and humour of the Pop Art movement to the realms of fashion illustration. Here was a style completely in tune with the rebellious clothes and free attitudes of the era. From the moment they were first published in *Women's Wear Daily* and *The New York Times* Antonio's drawings were much in demand, sought out by designers, stores and magazines around the world. Chameleon-like, he changed his colours with the years, skilfully adapting to the current mode, his extraordinary vitality and his exquisite draughtsmanship inspiring scores of imitators. For over twenty years Antonio remained the most consistently influential fashion illustrator, and his career bridges the gap between the 1960s and the renaissance of fashion illustration in the 1980s.

Anna Piaggi, the eccentrically chic muse of couturier Karl Lagerfeld, gave free rein to Antonio's stylistic diversity in *Vanity*, the Italian Condé Nast magazine of which she was a founding spirit in 1981. She was also responsible for promoting the witty social caricatures of the young French artist Hippolyte Romain, for whose mercilessly satirical pencil she herself would provide an ideal subject. Romain, who says curiosity is his strongest asset, always wanted to be a journalist: 'I was in awe of *Paris Match* correspondents, I would have loved to write but I wasn't good enough.' In 1980 Prosper Assouline, the editor of *La Mode en Peinture*, asked him to illustrate the fêtes at the Palace, a wild Montmartre nightclub. 'The idea fascinated me,' Romain recalls, 'because to me Le Palace is what Le Moulin Rouge was at the turn of the century. I see myself as an artist in the tradition of Toulouse-Lautrec, a witness of his times.' Besides being a regular on the fashion scene for *Vanity*, *La Mode en Peinture*, *Vogue Sport*, *Passion*, *Libération*, and *l'Express*, Romain covers music for *Rock and Folk*, sport for *Figaro*, food for *Gault Millau*, and culture for *La Croix* (a Catholic daily). He thinks of himself as a journalist who tells a story with sketches instead of words. Romain's drawings are far from innocent and many of them qualify as vitriolic. His vision of fashion editors, for instance, is very funny – but in a frightening and sobering way.

Below left: Paris collections. Sketch by Hippolyte Romain, 1982.

Below right: Fashion by Pour Toi, 1986. Wood-cut for 'Vanity' by François Berthoud.

So are his sketches of fashion groupies and designers, whose affectations he compares to those of eighteenth-century hairdressers. 'I sometimes like to mock the futility of certain fashion editors, the vanity of certain designers, and the whole inflated self-importance of their little universe,' says Romain. But he adds that he loves the fashion world, even if he does not take it seriously: 'It's an amusing world, but it's amazing how people who work in fashion lack a sense of humour.'

Under Alberto Nodolini's art direction *Vanity*'s editorial policy continues to favour illustrations, and concentrates on promoting more indigenous Italian talent. Nodolini, an admirer of the bizarre and imaginative work of the *fumetti* comic-strip magazine illustrators, invited a selection of them to interpret the work of fashion designers. With his encouragement and guidance such diverse artists as Lorenzo Mattotti and François Berthoud, both established stars of the *fumetti*, and Stefano Canulli, a theatre and haute-couture designer, have developed their own highly idiosyncratic styles and they now rank among today's leading fashion illustrators.

Mattotti's highly finished oil-pastel technique is a classical contrast to the bizarre characters and surreal *mises en scènes* depicted in his illustrations. 'The materials I use enable me to create a work that isn't just a fashion sketch, but a finished illustration in the tradition of fashion plates of the 20s and 30s,' explains

Below left: Fashion by Pour Toi, 1986. Cover design for 'Vanity' by François Berthoud.

Below right: Back-buttoning gaberdine coat-dress, hat and gloves by Krizia, Spring/ Summer 1986. Pastel drawing for 'Vanity' by Lorenzo Mattotti.

the artist. He believes that being an outsider as regards the fashion world has given him 'a sort of virginity that frees me from restrictive schemes'. At the same time Mattotti's experience of the *fumetti* has been very useful in this new field; it is from them that he derives the peculiar characterization of his models. Each of them is a character, 'because my drawing is always very narrative. In my fashion illustrations I try to simplify the composition, avoiding the introduction of too many elements that might distract attention from the subject. The point for me is not to describe the dress but to interpret and present the stylistic choice that lies behind it.'

François Berthoud uses the unusual technique of wood-cutting for his illustrations: 'I like engraving fashion plates because it is terribly paradoxical; using such a hard instrument, giving weight to each gesture, to render something as light, as evanescent as an article of clothing.' His discoverer, Alberto Nodolini, believes that Berthoud's talent 'is to know how to translate phenomena like Expressionism into a modern perspective. He makes them comprehensible even to the very young who perhaps have never heard of them.' Berthoud is happy to be a 'commercial' artist, preferring the immediate communication with a large

Fashion by Gérard, 1986. Woodcut for 'Vanity' by François Berthoud.

public that journalistic reproduction achieves to the 'solitary admiration' of the occasional art-gallery visitor.

Like *Vanity*, the French magazine *La Mode en Peinture* has promoted the work of an eclectic selection of talented young artists, who report on each season's collections with wit and originality: they include Pierre le Tan, Nadja, Hélène Tran, Ruben Alterio and Tony Viramontes. When Viramontes made his debut in the late 1970s his hard and direct style was a marked contrast to the prevailing soft pastel school of fashion illustration. He scored an immediate success, rapidly acquiring the kind of prestigious editorial commissions too often allocated to photographers, from *Lei* in Italy, *Vogue* in the USA, *The Face* in Britain, *Marie-Claire* and *Le Monde* in France. Viramontes has also worked with some of the most renowned names in fashion, including Yves Saint Laurent, Valentino, Claude Montana, and Rochas cosmetics. His striking images of strong, dominant women, smouldering and smokey-eyed, vibrate with New Wave energy and sensuality.

Viramontes does not like to be labelled an 'illustrator' and considers himself 'an artistic creator, a creator of ideas in images'. Goldy — the latest Italian version of Fiorucci — and Hanae Mori, the Japanese couturière, recently asked him to take on

Below left: Fashion by Azzedine Alaia, 1984. Illustration by Tony Viramontes.

Below centre: Charcoal study of Teri Toye, 1984, by Tony Viramontes.

Below right: Advertising campaign for Valentino Couture, 1984. Watercolour and pastel by Tony Viramontes.

the artistic direction of their companies, from the decoration of their boutiques to the design of their collections.

Tony Viramontes belongs to a new generation of artists who know how to capitalize on their talent. He has explored and mastered several techniques and styles, from drawing — direct and hard, supple and coloured — to video and painting with felt-tip markers over photographs. 'I look for new ideas because I like to be in a state of creative anxiety and insecurity,' says the artist. 'If I feel sure of myself I cannot be creative. I try to renew myself.' Viramontes' elegant art is fused with humour and fantasy; he finds his inspiration everywhere – in the street, in music and dance. 'It is extremes and contrasts that inspire me – an enormous lady in the street leading a tiny dog on a leash, for example. It is essential to capture the image; not a detail, not a garment or an expression, but an impression. Of the hundreds of sketches I might make for one drawing, it's almost always the first which states the essential.'

In Britain the once-staid pages of *Tatler* magazine have been enlivened by their multi-talented fashion director Michael Roberts, who has also recently been appointed design director at *Vogue*. Roberts' repertoire extends far beyond the simple knack of making clothes look good in pictures. He writes with an unparalleled venom; he orchestrates fashion shows; and he photographs with a taste for witty send-ups and high camp that has made him notorious for 'going

too far and getting away with it'. Roberts also draws and paints; his eye-catching, Fauve-like illustrations, often with a primitive African theme, are characterized by flat patterns or *découpages* and are painted in violent colour. He is particularly interested in the juxtaposition of illustrations and photographs. 'I think of my illustrations solely as a graphic device for depicting a particular fashion – they are more "images" than "illustrations",' says Roberts. 'There is a consistency of style in my drawings, despite their apparent disparities, but it is the designer's idea behind the clothes themselves that dictates what I make of them. I do not impose my own style of drawing over that idea.'

Michael Roberts also commissions disquietingly Freudian illustrations from Grizelda Holderness, a Zimbabwe-born artist for whom fashion illustration is 'an extension of my own work and one in which I am more relaxed and free with ideas'. 'In parading ourselves we walk the line between grandeur and ridicule,' says the artist, 'the bird of paradise wheezing upside-down under a blue plume or dancing in a circle of light on the forest floor is deadly serious, astonishingly beautiful and very funny.' Holderness believes that the designer's job is to be the first to sense the desire for a particular fashion before it exists and to bring it into reality, and that her role 'is to announce its arrival'.

Many fashion editors of magazines primarily devoted to photographic images find an artist most useful when a garment is not available to be photographed, or

Opposite
Two gouaches by Michael Roberts for 'Tatler'. Above: Harlequin knit shirt and trousers by Issey Miyake, Summer 1986. Below: Knitwear by Joseph Tricot, Summer 1984.

Below left: Fashion by Geoffrey Beene, 1985. Advertisement for Lou Lattimore, Dallas. Cutout and pastel drawing by Mats.

Below centre and right: Two 'Fall Forecast' drawings by Mats for American 'Vogue', Autumn 1986. New shapes by Geoffrey Beene (left) and Gianni Versace (right).

when the outstanding trends of a new fashion direction rather than an overall view need to be suggested. This situation arises regularly with their previews of international collections, several months before the clothes are available at retail outlets. From a mere description or a catwalk snapshot the artist can evoke both the garment and the mood of the coming season. The Swedish-born artist Mats Gustavson performs this role for American *Vogue* and the French *Marie-Claire*; dispensing with all superfluous details he concentrates on the essentials of cut and style. Mats' economical use of line and colour, and his innate understanding of fashion are the definitive elements of his dramatically graphic style.

Joe Eula, an American artist now under contract to Italian *Harper's Bazaar*, is a familiar figure at the international collections, frenziedly sketching as the models cavort down the catwalk. Eula's diverse career began in the 1950s, covering social and fashion events with Eugenia Sheppard for the *Herald Tribune*; later he worked with Ernestine Carter at the London *Sunday Times*. 'I was considered the fastest pencil in the field,' Eula recalls. 'A mannequin need only do her turn at a fashion show and voila! – an illustration!' The editors of *Harper's Bazaar* rightly believe that Eula's dynamic, impressionistic watercolours capture the essence of each designer's collection far more effectively than the standard catwalk polaroids favoured by other publications.

Rodger Duncan is a young American illustrator who also works at lightning speed and always with a live model. 'She is the drawing,' says the artist. 'I am

Below
Milan collections. Two watercolours by Joe Eula for 'Harper's Bazaar', Summer 1985. Left: Black and white outfits by Gianni Versace. Right: Silk shantung blouses and trousers by Gianfranco Ferré.

Opposite
Above: 'Snowdrops' hat by Givenchy, 1985. Two-dimensional drawing by Zoltan for 'Harper's Bazaar'. Photo by Peter Hutchings (London). Below left: Jacket and scarf by Mary Goff for Studio Creative, Spring 1986. Gouache by Rodger Duncan for 'Madame Figaro'. Below right: Fashion by Angelo Tarlazzi, 1983. Advertisement for Bergdorf Goodman. Pencil drawing by George Stavrinos.

attracted to fashion illustration as a form of personal expression, interpreting the mood of the model according to what she is wearing. She is a young, active woman, her gestures and movements inspire me, and because I work so fast she can always be caught in motion.' There is a shape and feeling in Duncan's dynamic brushstrokes and glowing gouache colours which, coupled with his ability to capture a likeness in just a few lines, is much appreciated by American *Vogue*. They regularly commission from him both fashion drawings and portraits of elegantly dressed socialites.

Advertising is another medium where the illustrator can assert a designer's or clothing store's image with greater freedom than within the technical confines of photography. The Hungarian-born artist Zoltan's exquisite series of three-dimensional photo-drawing montages for the esoteric Japanese designer Issey Miyake are an outstanding example. The prestigious Japanese department store and American 'specialty' clothing store have emerged as major patrons of contemporary fashion illustrators. French artist Hélène Majera's glamorous, air-brushed *tableaux de mode* are greatly admired by the Japanese; the Tokyo department store New Melsa annually commissions four poster designs from her, each representing one of the four seasons and its fashion trends in line and colour. George Stavrinos is an artist best known for bringing a heightened realism to fashion illustration; his most widely acclaimed works are his advertising campaigns for Barney's and Bergdorf Goodman in New York. His black-and-

white pencil drawings are characterized by meticulous detail, classical rendering and dramatic shading. Although highly representational, Stavrinos' work often contains elements of surprising surrealism and architectural detail.

Illustrators have always responded to changing tastes in fashion, in society and in art. In the past they have been strongly influenced by Impressionism, Cubism, Suprematism, Surrealism; and the evidence of these movements can still be seen in the work of today's youngest talents. Each illustrator has affinities with particular artists and styles – George Stavrinos with Maxfield Parrish and Art Deco; Mats Gustavson with Matisse; Antonio Lopez with Pop Art. But all are alive to the exciting possibilities of the present, assimilating and recreating in their illustrations the most contemporary phenomena – like multi-media experiments, laser and video. Asked to do a particular job, to record the passing fashion, the artists featured in this book regularly produce work that vastly transcends mere documentation. Their work is no less considerable, no less fine art, for being so eminently practical, decorative and informative. Designed only to catch the fleeting moment, these intensely personal images point the mood and spirit of today with a poignancy which photographs could never match.

Opposite
Wash drawing of Halston Knitwear, 1984, by
Tony Viramontes.

ALTERIO

Alterio's atmospheric pastel drawings convey a sense of movement but also of 'gravitas', as in the Spanish masters he admires. Among his influences he also lists 'the theatre, street-life and music' and perhaps this explains the emotional intensity of his work.

Opposite: Marc Bohan of Dior at a fitting before showing his Summer 1986 couture collection. Pastel drawing for 'La Mode en Peinture'.

Above: Publicity poster for the Paris Metro entitled 'Arrivée d'air chic', 1986.

Christian Lacroix of Patou at a
fitting before showing his
Summer 1986 couture
collection. Pastel drawing for
'La Mode en Peinture'.

Karl Lagerfeld of Chanel at a fitting before showing his Summer 1986 couture collection. Pastel drawing for 'La Mode en Peinture'.

Opposite: Paco Rabanne at a
fitting before showing his
Summer 1986 couture
collection. Pastel drawing for
'La Mode en Peinture'.

Above: Red satin 18th-century
'fauteuil'-style hat by Karl
Lagerfeld, Winter 1986. Pastel
drawing for 'La Mode en
Peinture'.

Avallone's young and punk-ish figures revel in richly textured fashion — furs, lamé, mesh — and wildly pose in frieze-like silhouette.

Fashion and pen and ink drawings by Avallone, 1986.

Fashion and pen and ink
drawings by Avallone, 1986.

Berthoud's woodcuts have a savage, sensual quality; their sombre atmosphere is charged with eroticism. His interest lies in 'the balance between the animal and the human'.

Opposite: Gold lamé evening dress by Thierry Mugler, Summer 1986. Woodcut for 'Emois'.

Left: Evening wear by Franco Moschino, Summer 1986. Woodcut for 'Emois'.

Chanel-inspired suits by Blumarine, Summer 1986. Woodcut for 'Vanity'.

Overleaf
Left: Kimono-sleeved overcoat by Krizia, Winter 1985. Woodcut for 'Vanity'. Right: Printed silk jacket by Missoni, Summer 1986. Woodcut for 'Vanity'.

33

Opposite: Cover design for 'Emois', 1986.

Above: Cover design for 'Vanity', September 1986.

STEFANO CANULLI

Silk taffeta evening dress by Roberto Capucci, 1985. Acrylic on xerox base.

Overleaf: Fashion by Stefano Canulli, 1985. Acrylic on xerox base.

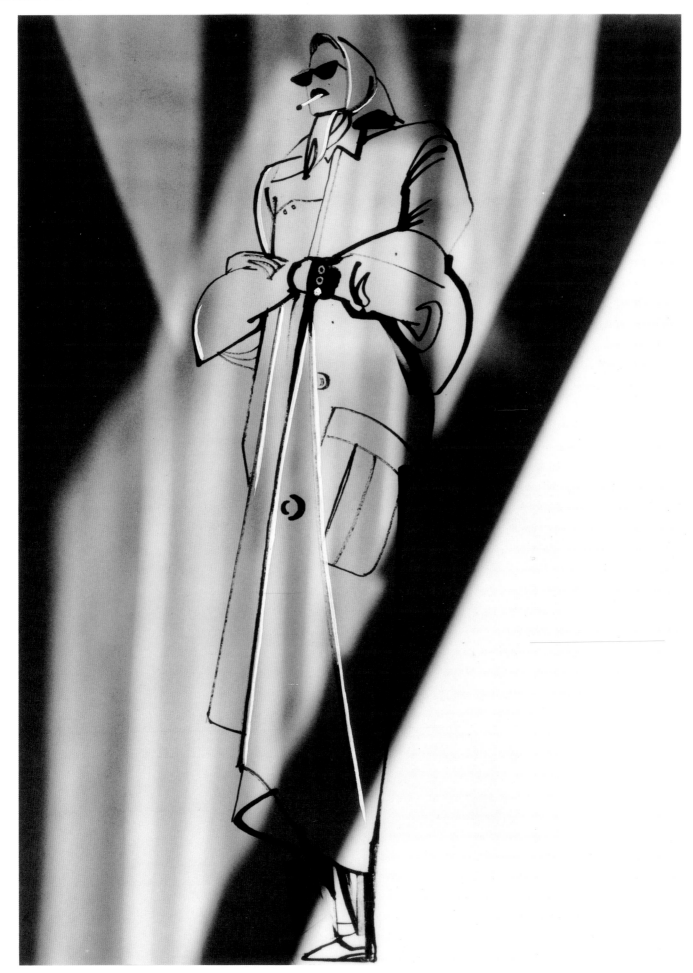

Michael Cooper

Cooper is a controversial young artist concerned with new ways of seeing. Playing with proportion, line and shadow, he creates striking images of timeless beauty. He sees his work as 'almost Cubist diagrammatical dissections of clothes — drawing through the clothes to show why they are beautiful in themselves'.

Opposite: Ink and shadow drawing for 'Dossier' magazine, 1987.

Left: Man in evening dress. Ink drawing, 1986.

Overleaf (left to right) Girl in sweater and black pants. Inkwash, 1986. Girl in white blouse and black skirt. Wax crayon and watercolour, 1986. Girl in orange tunic and black skirt. Wax crayon and watercolour, 1986.

The outstanding characteristic of Duncan's work is his use of blocks of high-voltage colour. His figures are free and easy, yet still sophisticated, and with an undercurrent of energy concealed beneath a deceptively relaxed poise.

Opposite: Red satin evening trenchcoat by Ralph Lauren, 1985. Gouache for American 'Vogue'.

Above: Turban by Stephen Jones, 1985. Gouache for American 'Vogue'.

Right: Yellow blouse by Patrick Kelly, 1985. Gouache for American 'Vogue'.

Opposite: Black peplum jacket and white hat by Olies D'elodie, Spring 1986. Gouache for 'Madame Figaro'.

Above: Publicity poster for American 'Vogue', 1986. Gouache.

*Opposite: Portrait of
Wilhelmina van Souest, 1986.*

*Left: Evening dress by Carolina
Herrera, 1986. Gouache for
American 'Vogue'.*

Reporting on international fashion shows Eula manages, with a few rapid strokes of his paintbrush, to reproduce the line, colour and cut of an outfit in the short time that it takes for a model to parade the catwalk.

Above: Paris collections. Yves Saint Laurent Rive Gauche, Summer 1984. Watercolour for 'Harper's Bazaar'.

Right: Milan collections. Basile, Summer 1984. Watercolour for 'Harper's Bazaar'.

61

Fashion by Yves Saint Laurent, Winter 1986. Watercolour for 'Harper's Bazaar'.

Fashion by Karl Lagerfeld, Winter 1986. Watercolour for 'Harper's Bazaar'.

Left: Knitwear by Missoni, Summer 1985. Watercolour for 'Harper's Bazaar'.

Opposite: Evening dress by Chanel, Winter 1984. Watercolour for 'Harper's Bazaar'.

July 89   Paris

Paris/85

Opposite
Left: Fashion by Yves Saint
Laurent, Winter 1985.
Watercolour for 'Harper's
Bazaar'. Right: Fashion by
Claude Montana, Winter
1985. Watercolour for 'Harper's
Bazaar'.

Above: Fashion by Givenchy,
1985. Watercolour for 'Harper's
Bazaar'.

Right: Fashion by Gianni
Versace, 1985. Watercolour for
'Harper's Bazaar'.

Holderness's pictures of women have a disquietingly Freudian quality. She sees them as capable, independent, mysterious as animals — behaving according to some secret law — and, as animals are, elusive, beautiful, flighty, innocent, knowing and preoccupied.

Opposite: 'Birdwalk' — evening ensembles by Yves Saint Laurent Rive Gauche, Winter 1983. Pastel drawing for 'Tatler'.

Above: 'Boardwalk' — evening ensembles by Valentino, Winter 1983. Pastel drawing for 'Tatler'.

Overleaf: 'The Age of Reason' — Yves Saint Laurent beatnik look for Rive Gauche, Winter 1985. Pastel drawing for 'Tatler'.

GRIZELDA HOLDERNESS

'Evening Activities' – African-
influenced Summer outfits by
Kenzo (seated left), and Issey
Miyake, 1984. Pastel drawing
for 'Tatler'.

Overleaf: 'Fashion Slaves' – on
the left, Claude Montana's
orange fur and zebra stripes; on
the right, Karl Lagerfeld's
giant-candelabra-embroidered
evening dress, Winter 1985.
Pastel drawing for 'Tatler'.

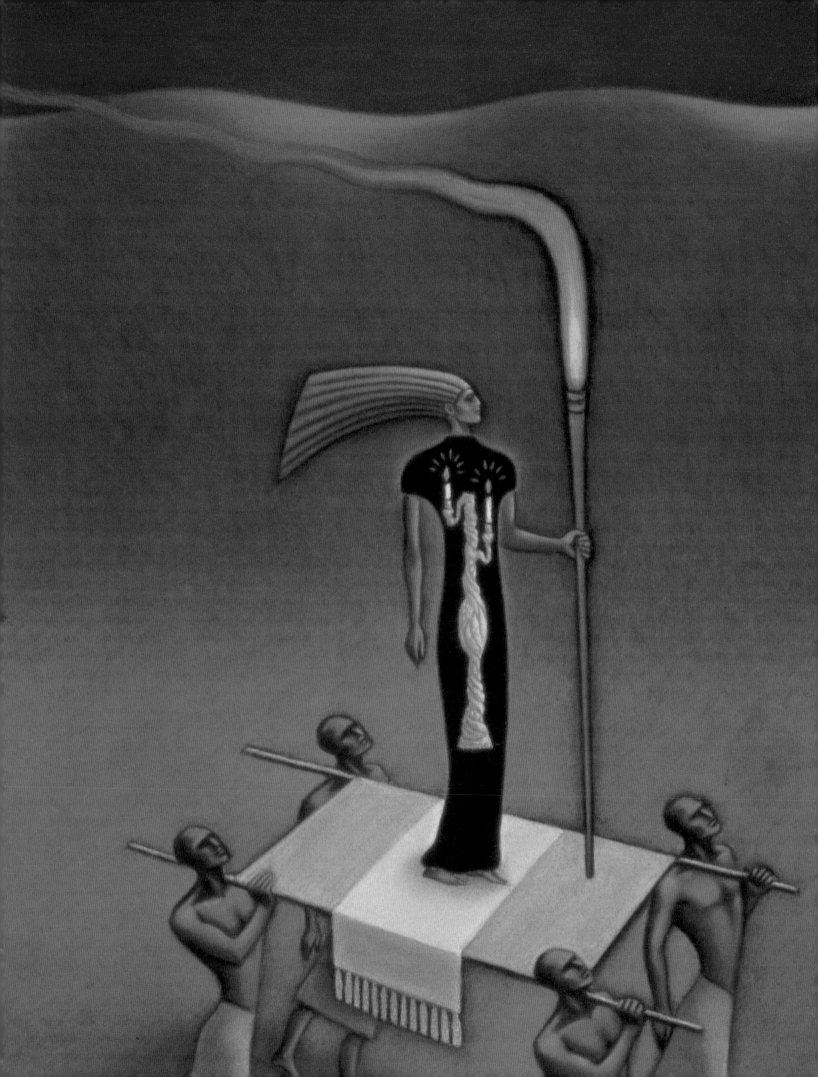

Le Tan's style looks back to the Paris of the 1930s and 40s – the charmed world of Christian Bérard and Jean Cocteau, Pavel Tchelitchev and Cecil Beaton. In their lightness of touch his pen-and-wash drawings have something of pre-war wit and elegance.

Opposite: Four ink and gouache illustrations of hat designs for 'Madame Figaro', 1985.

Dalmatian-spotted hat and black-and-white suit by Jean-Paul Gaultier, Winter 1984. Gouache for 'La Mode en Peinture'.

Above: Safari jacket by Marithé and François Girbaud; skirt by Gaston Jaunet; hat by Tokio Kumagai, Summer 1984. Gouache for 'La Mode en Peinture'.

Opposite: Chanel golfing suit, Summer 1984. Ink and gouache for 'La Mode en Peinture'.

Le golf

L.-T.

Left: Poster for the Jelmoli
department store, Lyons, France,
1984. Watercolour and pastel
drawing.

Above: Poster for the New
Melsa department store, Tokyo,
Spring 1985. Watercolour and
pastel drawing.

'Body-building' — poster for
Mure-Blanc publishers, Paris
1983. Ink and pastel drawing.

MATS

Mats catches the essence of a garment using a few bold and simple lines: dispensing with all superfluous detail he concentrates on the essentials of cut, colour and style. His power is of suggestion, rather than description.

Opposite: Evening dress by Geoffrey Beene, 1984. Advertisement for Lou Lattimore, Dallas. Pastel drawing.

Right: Dress by Azzedine Alaia, Autumn 1985. Cut-out and chalk drawing for 'Marie-Claire Bis'.

Opposite: Evening dress by Karl
Lagerfeld, 1983. Advertisement
for Lou Lattimore, Dallas.
Pastel drawing.

Above: Beauty illustration,
1985. Pastel drawing for
'Marie-Claire Bis'.

Overleaf
Two pastel drawings for
'Marie-Claire Bis', Autumn
1984. Left: Suit and coat by
Azzedine Alaia. Right: Outfit
by Issey Miyake.

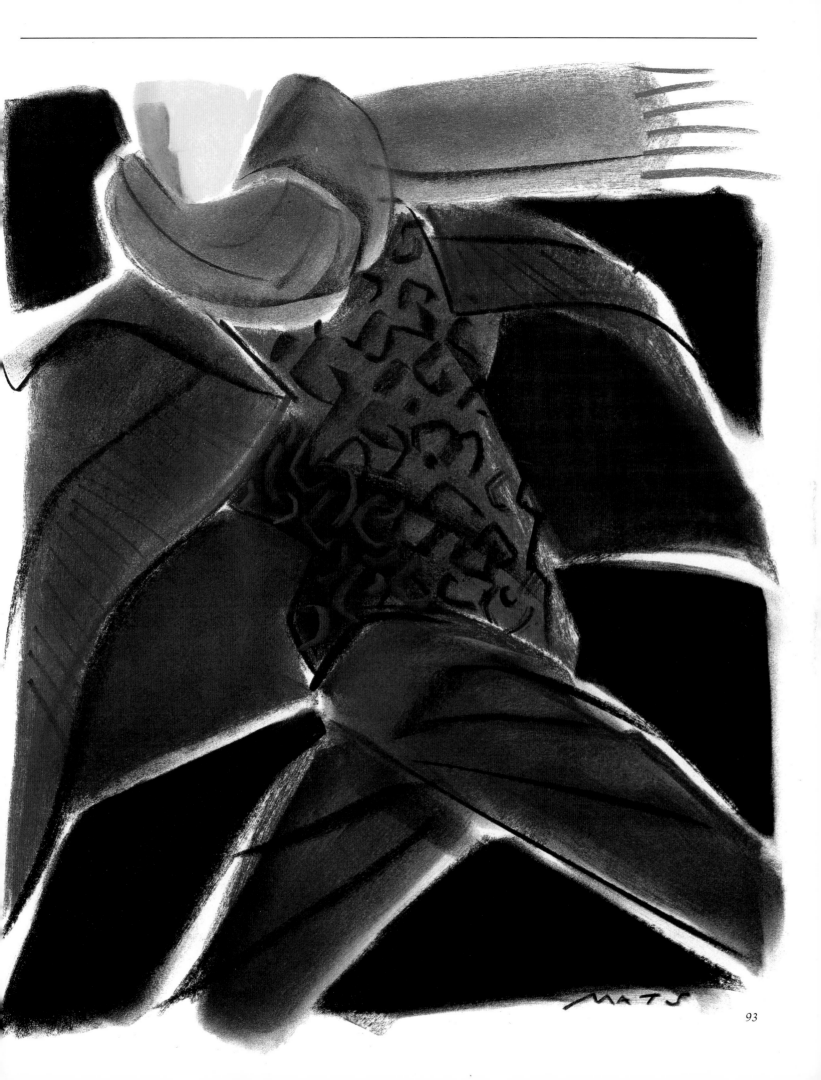

Suit by Jean-Paul Gaultier, Autumn 1984. Pastel drawing for 'Marie-Claire Bis'.

Dress and hooded scarf by Azzedine Alaia, Autumn 1984. Pastel drawing for 'Marie-Claire Bis'.

MATS

Mattotti began his career as a 'fumetti' illustrator and his dramatic fashion drawings reflect this fact. His figures are unearthly, their faces enigmatic masks, and the situations depicted are mysterious and unexplained.

Opposite: Missoni dress and cotton jacket (left); Fendi denim dress (right). Pastel drawing for 'Vanity', 1986.

Above: Black printed velvet coat by Gianni Versace. Pastel drawing for 'Vanity', 1985.

Following pages Fashion by Jil Sander. Pastel drawing for 'Vanity', 1985.

Left and right: Two silk taffeta outfits by Coveri. Pastel drawings for 'Vanity', 1985.

Lawrence Mynott

Whether his subject is bathing belles or the latest
'folie' from Chanel, Mynott brings a whimsical
touch to his allusive drawings, be they a witty
'hommage' to Jean Cocteau or a glamorous
emulation of the 1950s high-style
of René Gruau.

*Paris ready-to-wear collections,
Winter 1986. Opposite:
Comme des Garçons. Right:
Hermès. Ink drawings for 'The
Observer'.*

an alarming one piece costume......

Stephen Jones' charming beach hat.

Two pen and gouache drawings
for 'The Observer', Summer
1986. Top: Black and white
striped bathing suit by Rifat
Ozbeck. Above: Two-blues
cotton beach hat by Stephen
Jones.

Right: Paris couture collections,
Winter 1986. Fashion by (left
to right) Yves Saint Laurent,
Emanuel Ungaro, Karl
Lagerfeld for Chanel, Christian
Lacroix for Jean Patou.
Gouache for 'The Observer'.

2.

Nadja

In her fashion illustrations Nadja creates dramatic 'mises-en-scène' in which beautiful women prepare themselves for passionate nights. Her fashion portraits are characterized by distortion and a bizarre perspective.

Opposite: Leopard-print dress and green taffeta turban by Yves Saint Laurent, couture collection, Winter 1983. Dry pastel for 'La Mode en Peinture'.

Above: Hat by Jean-Charles Brousseau, 1985. Fashion portrait for 'Illustration'.

Overleaf
Left: Black velvet and white crêpe evening dress by Yves Saint Laurent, couture collection, Winter 1983. Dry pastel for 'La Mode en Peinture'. Right: Short, black lace, sequinned evening dress with red taffeta sleeves and feathered hat by Yves Saint Laurent, couture collection, Winter 1983. Dry pastel for 'La Mode en Peinture'.

Above: Black velvet and taffeta cocktail dress and hat by Yves Saint Laurent, couture collection, Winter 1983. Dry pastel for 'La Mode en Peinture'.

Opposite: Brown wool coat and fur-brimmed hat by Yves Saint Laurent, couture collection, Winter 1983. Dry pastel for 'La Mode en Peinture'.

Michael Roberts

Roberts is a phenomenon: writer, photographer, editor and artist. His outrageous sense of style and venomous pen have made him the fashion world's perennial 'enfant terrible'.

Two gouaches for 'Tatler', 1986. Opposite: Liza Bruce's shirred black swimsuit with cut-outs. Above: Liza Bruce's shirred stripey swimsuit and half-and-half two-piece.

Overleaf
Four gouaches for 'Tatler', 1984. From left to right: Madras checked cotton skirt and T-shirt by Fenn Wright & Manson. Cotton top and zoave trousers by John McIntyre. Leopard angora robe by Ninivah Khomo. Black and yellow cotton skirt from Magenta.

British ready-to-wear collections, Winter 1986. Charcoal drawings for 'Tatler'. Opposite: David Fielden's black velvet dress with blue flocked taffeta bustle. Right: Tom Bell's brown silk jersey off-the-shoulder dress with black silk braiding.

The Chanel ready-to-wear
show, Summer 1985. Pencil
and watercolour for 'Vanity'.

Overleaf
Left: Red linen toga dress by
Gianni Versace, jewellery by
Ugo Correani, Summer 1983.
Pencil and watercolour for
'Vanity' of the Italian ready-to-
wear collections. Right: Paris
fashion groupies at the
Tuileries, Autumn 1985. Pencil
and watercolour for 'Vanity'.

George Stavrinos (signature)

Stavrinos' work is lushly representational — classical in line and dramatic in shading, suggesting nostalgia and romance in its allusive imagery. His drawings seem to emerge from a dream which we all share, where everything is perfect and everyone is beautiful.

Three advertisements for Bergdorf Goodman, 1983. Above left: Fashion by Angelo Tarlazzi. Graphite pencil drawing for the 'New York Sunday Times'. Below left: Suit by Azzedine Alaia. Graphite pencil drawing for American 'Vogue'. Right: Lynx fur coat. Graphite pencil drawing for American 'Vogue'.

Right: Advertisement for Bergdorf Goodman, 1983, published in American 'Vogue'. Graphite pencil drawing.

Above left: 'Woman with six portraits' — advertisement for Bergdorf Goodman, 1980, published in the 'New York Sunday Times'. Graphite pencil drawing.

Below left: 'Figure with sculpture' — advertisement for Bergdorf Goodman, 1979, published in 'W' magazine. Graphite pencil drawing.

Above: 'Ladies in black leather' — advertisement for Mauricius clothing store, Dusseldorf, 1984. Graphite pencil drawing.

Opposite: 'The Round Window' — fashion by Mary McFadden, 1980. Editorial for the 'New York Times' magazine. Graphite pencil drawing.

'The Letter' – advertisement for Bergdorf Goodman, 1979. Graphite pencil drawing.

Opposite: 'The Spell' – fashion by Valentino, 1981. Advertisement for Bergdorf Goodman, published in the 'New York Sunday Times'. Graphite pencil drawing.

Steven Stipelman

A true professional, Stipelman can report on the international collections, preview a celebrity's 'new look' for 'Women's Wear Daily' or sum up a cosmetic firm's seasonal programme, all with uncanny accuracy and flair.

Opposite: Camel-hair coat by Ralph Lauren. Cover design for 'Women's Wear Daily', December 1985. Gouache and crayon.

Above: Alpaca-knit shawl-collar coat and bodysuit by Donna Karan. Cover design for 'Women's Wear Daily', December 1985. Gouache and crayon.

Overleaf
Left: Suit by Oscar de la Renta. Cover design for 'Women's Wear Daily', December 1985. Gouache and crayon. Right: Suit by Bill Blass. Cover design for 'Women's Wear Daily', December 1985. Gouache and crayon.

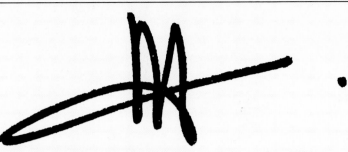

Tran's ideal woman — elegant, subtle and intelligent, with a glamour and humour 'à la Schiaparelli' — is brought vividly to life in her wittily theatrical watercolours and pastel drawings.

Opposite: Striped raincoat, white wool skirt and cashmere and silk printed waistcoat, all by Hermès, Summer 1986. Ink and watercolour for 'La Mode en Peinture'.

Above: Illustration for the subscriptions page of 'La Mode en Peinture', 1986. Ink and watercolour.

Overleaf
Left: Skirt, blouse and belt by Anne-Marie Beretta, Summer 1986. Ink and watercolour for 'La Mode en Peinture'. Right: Long navy panne velvet evening dress by Yves Saint Laurent, couture collection, Winter 1985. Ink and watercolour for 'La Mode en Peinture'.

Yves Saint Laurent

Robe de Soir long de femme
de Velours Marine

VIRAMONTES

Left: Embroidered evening suit with sable edging by Karl Lagerfeld for Chanel Couture, Winter 1984. Watercolour for 'La Mode en Peinture'.

Opposite: Illustration for a T-shirt design.

Opposite: Valentino beauté, 1984.

Above left: Yves Saint Laurent smoking suit, 1984. Above right and below right: Two illustrations for an advertising campaign for Valentino couture, 1984. Watercolour. Below left: Fashion by Perry Ellis.

Details of illustrations on previous page.

Opposite: Beauty portrait for 'Marie-Claire Beauté'.

Purple tunic and skirt by Judith & Company, Autumn 1986. Gouache advertisement by Rodger Duncan for Jordan Marsh in American 'Vogue'.

RUBEN ALTERIO

Ruben Alterio was born in 1949 in Buenos Aires, where he studied art at the Beaux-Arts school, before moving to Paris in 1976. Since 1980 Alterio has been a freelance illustrator, contributing regularly to *Marie-Claire* and *La Mode en Peinture*.
He lists Goya, Velazquez, Delacroix, Matisse, De Stael and Bacon among his influences, as well as 'the theatre, street-life, and music'. Alterio held an exhibition of his paintings in Paris in 1987.
Contact: Sylvie Flaure and Georges Said, 20 rue Chalgrin, 75116 Paris. Tel: 45 00 44 00.

GENNARO AVALLONE

Avallone was born in 1955 in the province of Salerno, Southern Italy. He studied art and design for two years at the Scuola d'Arte Applicata in Milan, then went on to do a three-year course of Graphic Design at the Istituto per l'Arte e il Restauro in Florence, from which he obtained a diploma.
He was subsequently with a firm of graphic designers in Rome and now works freelance – for the most part in Rome and Milan. Since he has turned his hand to fashion illustration, his drawings have been published in several magazines, including *Zoom* and *Fashion* in Italy, as well as *Vogue* and *Follow Me* in Australia.
Contact: S.G.L.U., Via Giannone 2, 20154 Milan. Tel: (02) 316427

Above: Dress by Issey Miyake, Autumn 1984. Pastel drawing by Ruben Alterio for 'La Mode en Peinture'. Right: Fashion and pen and ink drawing by Gennaro Avallone, 1986.

FRANÇOIS BERTHOUD

François Berthoud was born in Switzerland in 1961 and studied illustration in Lausanne.

After receiving his diploma in 1982 he moved to Milan and began working for Condé Nast, and for the *fumetti* comic-strip magazines. Within a year he was appointed art director of *Vogue Sposa*. He is now one of the principal contributors to *Vanity* magazine, designing nearly all their covers as well as illustrating numerous editorial features.

Berthoud divides his time between Paris and Milan, contributing to many leading international publications: in Italy, *Linus*, *Alter Alter*, *Per Lui*, *Vogue Bambini*, *Vogue* and *Alfabeta*; in Germany, *Manner Vogue*; in France, *Globe* and *Emois*. He has also created animated cartoons for Italian television (RAI), and has held exhibitions at Prato (the Italian Textiles Fair) and at the Paris 'Jeunes Createurs' fashion shows in Autumn 1986.

Contact: François Berthoud, 81 rue des Archives, 75003 Paris. Tel: 42 72 08 77.
Or: 22 Corso XXII Marzo, Milan. Tel: (02) 58 62 78.
Agent: Claudine Serre, 27 rue Rémy Dumoncel, 75014 Paris. Tel: 42 09 96 88.

Left: Cover design for 'Vanity', 1986, by François Berthoud.

Opposite
Left: Illustration for 'Easter bonnets' fashion feature in the 'New York Times' magazine, 1980, by Harvey Boyd. Right: Fashion and acrylic painting by Stefano Canulli, 1985.

HARVEY BOYD

Harvey Boyd was born in Connecticut in 1941, and he attended Parsons School of Design in New York from 1960 to 1964. He worked in the art departments of Fabergé and Estée Lauder cosmetics, before his talent attracted the attention of the *Los Angeles Times* fashion editor, who invited him to Europe. He credits that first transatlantic experience with providing broader exposure for his work. His illustrations have now decorated the pages of American fashion's most powerful voices – *Women's Wear Daily, Vogue* and *The New York Times* – as well as appearing in *Elle, Self, Flair, Essence, Mademoiselle, Gentleman's Quarterly*, and *Harper's Bazaar*.

Boyd has illustrated promotions for Yves Saint Laurent, Perry Ellis, Diane von Fürstenburg, Valentino and Daniel Hechter. He has also designed fabrics and assisted Fernando Sanchez with performance costumes for Mick Jagger of the Rolling Stones. He currently holds joint teaching posts at the Fashion Institute of Technology and at Parsons School of Design in New York. Boyd has held one-man exhibitions in New York and Miami and now concentrates on painting large-scale semi-abstract pictures.

Contact: Harvey Boyd, 24 5th Avenue, New York, New York 10011. Tel: (212) 475 5235.

STEFANO CANULLI

Stefano Canulli was born in Rome in 1959. After completing his studies in figurative art at the Roman Lyceum of Arts, he went on to study art history at the Academy of Fashion and Costume. He also attended various photography and cinema courses in Rome. At nineteen he began working as an assistant to the costume designer on various Italian films, on major shows produced by the Italian television network (RAI) and for several Roman fashion houses.

As a designer and illustrator Canulli has collaborated with Piero Tosi and Mauro Pagano on opera and theatre projects. He is now the official illustrator to the couture house of Roberto Capucci, as well as illustrating promotions for Valentino and Bruno Piatelli, and he regularly contributes to *Vanity*.

Contact: Stefano Canulli, Via della Tribuna di Campitelli 9, int. 2, 00186 Rome.

MICHAEL COOPER

Michael Cooper was born in Toronto, Canada in 1963. He studied art at the Ryerson Polytechnical Institute and at the age of eighteen was already working as a fashion illustrator for the Toronto department stores Creed's, Harridge's, and Holt Renfrew.

In 1982 he moved to New York and enrolled at the Fashion Institute of Technology. After illustrating a fashion book for Marisa Berenson, he won his first account, with the Brooklyn specialty store 'Jimmy's'; then in 1985 he began working for Bergdorf Goodman and has since done all their fashion advertising in *The New York Times*.

Cooper admires the work of Picasso and Man Ray.

Contact: Michael Cooper, 87 Crosby Street, New York, New York 10012. Tel: (212) 226 6733.

RODGER DUNCAN

Rodger Duncan was born in Bucks County, Pennsylvania and studied fine art at the Pennsylvania Academy of Arts. He received his masters degree after a year of studying painting in Florence. The artists he most admires are Picasso and Matisse, for their sense of colour and shape.

His first commissions were advertisements for department stores, and he has since worked for designers Calvin Klein, Oscar de la Renta, Chanel and Ann Klein, and for *Harper's Bazaar*, *New York* magazine and American *Vogue*, to which he is a regular contributor.

Contact: Rodger Duncan, 425 Park Avenue South, New York, New York. Tel: (212) 532 0966.

Agent: Jean Gabriel Kauss, 122 E 42nd Street, New York, New York 10168. Tel: (212) 370 4300.

Left: Ink and dye drawing by Michael Cooper, 1986. Above: Private portrait study of the singer Marilyn, 1986. Gouache by Rodger Duncan.

JOE EULA

Joe Eula's career began in the 1950s, covering social and fashion events with Eugenia Sheppard for the *Herald Tribune*, and later with Ernestine Carter at the London *Sunday Times*. Eula also created posters and portraits for many celebrities, including Miles Davis, Marlene Dietrich, Diana Vreeland, and later the Supremes and Liza Minnelli.

In the 1960s he shared a studio with photographer Milton Greene, collaborating on covers, news and fashion stories for *Life* magazine. When their partnership ended in 1968 Eula began designing sets and costumes for George Balanchine and Jerome Robbins at the New York City Ballet, and for the theatre, winning a Tony Award for his work on a Broadway production of *Private Lives* in 1968. Eula also directed television 'fashion specials' for film stars, including Candice Bergen and Lauren Bacall.

In the 1970s he worked with the designer Halston; produced illustrations for *Vogue* magazine; and worked on Diana Vreeland's costume shows at the Metropolitan Museum of Art, until signing an exclusive contract with Italian and French *Harper's Bazaar* in 1979.

Contact: Joe Eula, 41 West 54th Street, New York, New York 10019. Tel: (212) 582 4725.

GRIZELDA HOLDERNESS

Grizelda Holderness was born in Harare, Zimbabwe, in 1953. She came to England in 1972 and attended Bristol School of Art from 1972–73 and the Central School of Art and Design in London from 1973–76.

She has designed book jackets for Pan, Picador, Penguin, Corgi and Dent, and in 1983 she won the Pan Young Illustrator of the Year award. She regularly contributes illustrations to magazines, including *Tatler, Vanity Fair, Cosmopolitan, Working Woman, Gentleman's Quarterly, Woman's Journal, Sunday Times* Magazine and *New Scientist*.

Grizelda Holderness has had three solo exhibitions at the Thumb Gallery in London.

Contact: c/o Thumb Gallery, 20/21 D'Arblay Street, London W1V 3NF. Tel: (01) 434 2931.

Above: Outfits by Complice, 1985. Watercolour for 'Harper's Bazaar' by Joe Eula. Right: 'Boardwalk' – evening ensembles by Valentino, Winter 1983. Pastel drawing for 'Tatler' by Grizelda Holderness.

PIERRE LE TAN

Pierre le Tan was born in Paris in 1950. The son of an artist, he received no formal training.

His first notable commission was one of many subsequent cover designs for *The New Yorker* magazine in 1969. He has worked for numerous other American publications, including *The New York Times*, *Time*, *Harper's Bazaar*, *Atlantic Monthly* and *Holiday*, as well as illustrating many books and book jackets.

He was first asked to illustrate fashion in 1982 by the editor of *La Mode en Peinture*, for whom he has continued to work while also contributing both fashion drawings and portraits of fashion personalities to *Madame Figaro* and *Tatler* magazines.

In 1983 he designed the sets and costumes for *La Chiène d'Actilographe*, a play about a Paris fashion house during the Second World War. He has recently written and illustrated a volume of imaginary memoirs of international café society, *Rencontres d'une Vie, 1945-1984*.

Contact: Pierre le Tan, 4 rue St Augustin, 75002 Paris. Tel: 42 97 50 09.

HÉLÈNE MAJERA

Hélène Majera was born in 1944 in the Pyrenees region of France. She studied art at the Lycée Technique Ganneron in Paris.

From 1962 to 1969 she worked at the Nouvelles Galeries graphic arts studio, until becoming a freelance illustrator in 1970. Her work has appeared in numerous international publications, including *Marie-Claire*, *Harper's Bazaar*, *La Mode en Peinture*, *Votre Beauté*, *GAP*, *Dépêche Mode* and *Cosmopolitan*. Hélène Majera specializes in publicity posters, both in France and Japan, and her clients include the Printemps and Jelmoli department stores and Rochas perfumes in France, and the New Melsa department store in Japan.

She has taken part in many group exhibitions: the Salon d'Automne, Figuration Critique, Look Rock, *La Mode en Peinture* at the Espace Cardin and Images et Imaginaires d'Architecture at the Beaubourg, as well as holding a solo exhibition at the Parisian Galerie Huit in 1986. Her posters have won awards from organizations as varied as the Art Director's Club of Tokyo, Japan Railways, and the Grand Prix de l'Affiche Française (both in 1977 and 1984).

Contact: Hélène Majera, 13 rue Pelée, 75011 Paris. Tel: 48 06 65 21.

Left: Ink and gouache illustration of a hat design for 'Madame Figaro' 1985, by Pierre Le Tan. Above: Poster for the New Melsa department store, Tokyo, Winter 1981. Graphite and watercolour by Hélène Majera.

MATS

Mats Gustavson was born in Sweden in 1951. From 1970 to 1974 he studied at the National College of Fine Arts in Stockholm. After designing costumes for films and television he returned to college in 1976, graduating in Costume and Stage Design from the Scandinavian Drama Institute.

He began working freelance as a fashion illustrator for Swedish magazines and stores and his first work commissioned by an international magazine was for British *Vogue* in 1978; this was soon followed by commissions from American *Vogue* and *Marie-Claire* in France. In 1980 he moved to New York and now divides his time between that city and Paris. He continues to work internationally for Condé Nast publications in America, Britain, France, Germany, Italy and Australia, as well as *Interview* and *The New York Times* in America, and *Marie-Claire* and *Marie-Claire Bis* in France.

Other projects include promotions for Bergdorf Goodman, Bloomingdale's, Henri Bendel, Printemps, Revlon, Lancôme, Chanel, L'Oréal, and Geoffrey Beene. Mats was commissioned by the Council of Fashion Designers of America (CFDA) in 1984 and 1985 to execute portraits of designers honoured by them.

Contact: Art & Commerce, 108 West 18th Street, New York, New York 10011. Tel: (212) 206 0737.

Pastel portrait of Diana Vreeland, 1984, by Mats.

LORENZO MATTOTTI

Lorenzo Mattotti was born in 1954. He studied architecture in Venice, later turning to illustration, and he has become one of the leading figures in the renaissance of the *fumetti* comic-strip magazines.

His work has appeared in many international publications, including *Linus, Alter Alter, Frigidair, Metal Hurlant, L'Echo des Savanes, The Face, Escape* and *Raw*. He has published comic books in both France and Italy: *Alice brum brum, Tram Tram Rock, Huckleberry Finn, Il Signor Spartaco, Incidenti* and *Fuochi*, which won the prize of Best International Work at the 1986 comics convention in Barcelona. In the field of children's illustration, his work regularly appears in the *Corriere dei Piccoli* and he has published a book, *El Hombre Que . . .*, in Spain.

With the encouragement of Alberto Nodolini, Mattotti has also taken up fashion illustration and he is now one of the main contributors to *Vanity*.

Contact: Lorenzo Mattotti, Via Ragusa 8, Milan. Tel: (02) 602 957/ 376 3013.

Above: Dress by Cadette. Pastel drawing by Lorenzo Mattotti for 'Vanity', 1985. Opposite: Chanel suit. Brush and ink drawing by Lawrence Mynott for 'The Observer', Autumn 1986.

LAWRENCE MYNOTT

Lawrence Mynott was born in London in 1954. He studied art at Chelsea School of Art from 1972 to 1976, and illustration at the Royal College of Art from 1976 to 1979.

Since then Mynott has worked as a freelance illustrator specializing in figurative work, portraiture and fashion. His work has appeared in many British publications, including *Tatler, Vogue, Harper's & Queen*, the *Observer* and the *Radio Times*, as well as *La Mode en Peinture* and *Madame Figaro* in France.

He has also designed numerous book jackets, many for Penguin books, and was awarded the 1984 Designer's and Art Director's Silver Award for the best series of book jackets. He has held two one-man portraiture shows at the Cale Gallery in London.

Contact: Lawrence Mynott, 23 Mount Port Road, London W5. Tel: (01) 997 8376.

NADJA

Nadja Fejto was born in 1955 in Alexandria and she has lived in France since 1960.

A self-taught artist, Nadja concentrated on personal work between 1970 and 1980. Since then she has worked as a freelance illustrator, contributing to the magazines *Palace, La Mode en Peinture* and *Vanity*.

Her favourite artists are Toulouse-Lautrec and Degas. Nadja has published a children's book and a book of erotic drawings.

Contact: Nadja Fejto, 34 bis rue Amelot, 75011 Paris. Tel: 48 06 51 40.

MICHAEL ROBERTS

Michael Roberts studied graphic and fashion design at High Wycombe College of Art.

His original intention was to become an art director at J. Walter Thompson, but instead he became a freelance fashion illustrator, working for publications including the *Sunday Times, Nova, Vingt Ans* and *Vogue* (UK). He joined the *Sunday Times* as fashion editor in 1972 and nine years later became fashion editor of *Tatler* magazine. In 1983 he moved to *Vanity Fair* in New York, but returned the following year to *Tatler* as Fashion Director. In 1986 he was also appointed Design Director of *Vogue* (UK).

Roberts admires the work of Picasso and Primitive African art.

Contact: Michael Roberts, Condé Nast Publications Ltd, Vogue House, Hanover Square, London W1R 0AD. Tel: (01) 499 9080.

Left: Fashion portrait with Yves Saint Laurent hat, Winter 1983. Dry pastel by Nadja. Above: Swimsuit by Liza Bruce, Summer 1986. Gouache by Michael Roberts for 'Tatler'.

HIPPOLYTE ROMAIN

Hippolyte Romain was born in Paris in 1947. He originally intended to be a journalist but found he was better at drawing than writing. He taught himself to draw by going to museums and copying the work of Toulouse-Lautrec, Utrillo and other painters of the turn of the century. Meanwhile, in order to earn a living he was a door-to-door salesman, gave boxing lessons, and ran a restaurant where he doubled as a chef.

In 1980 the editor of *La Mode en Peinture* asked him to illustrate the fêtes at the Palace nightclub and Romain's career took off. Anna Piaggi published many of his drawings in *Vanity* and he is now a regular on the fashion scene for *La Mode en Peinture, Vogue Sport, Passion, Libération* and *l'Express*; he covers music for *Rock and Folk*, food for *Gault Millau*, and culture for *La Croix*. He has also been a war correspondent in Beirut, and has done a series of drawings for the German magazine *Stern* and two series for American *Vanity Fair* — for the latter, his subject was the brothels of Singapore. He has published a comic-strip book *Ces Chéries* and a compilation of his *Reportages*.

Contact: Hippolyte Romain, 5 rue Lapeyrère, 75018 Paris. Tel: 42 59 30 33.

TIM SHEAFFER

Tim Sheaffer was born in Wilmington, Delaware, and studied at the Rhode Island School of Design.

After moving to Manhattan, he began his career as a freelance fashion illustrator. His deliciously witty caricatures of New York's fashion and society celebrities won instant acclaim, and comparisons were made with such legendary caricaturists as the Belle Epoque Parisian Fem. As well as promotions for Bergdorf Goodman, Henri Bendel and the Trump Tower, Sheaffer's work regularly appears in *Vanity Fair* and the American, British and German editions of *Vogue*.

Contact: Keeble Cavaco and Duka Inc, 853 Seventh Avenue, New York, NY 10019 Tel: (212) 582 3473.

Above: Swimming costume by Karl Lagerfeld for Fendi, Summer 1983. Pencil and watercolour by Hippolyte Romain for 'Vanity'. Right: Unpublished fashion portrait, 1986, by Tim Sheaffer.

GEORGE STAVRINOS

George Stavrinos was born in 1948 in Somerville, Massachusetts. He studied graphic art at the Rhode Island School of Design and spent a year pursuing independent study in Italy.

In 1973 Stavrinos moved to New York and became a freelance illustrator. His first client was *The New York Times*; this led to jobs for *New York* magazine, Bonwit Teller, Columbia Records, and Pan Am, and fashion illustrations for the magazine *Gentleman's Quarterly*. Two years of steady fashion illustration work for Barney's menswear store followed. From Barney's he went on in 1979 to produce a widely acclaimed campaign for Bergdorf Goodman.

In 1984 he began drawing advertisements for Beverly Sill's New York Opera, as well as a series of advertisements for architectural projects, portraits for magazines, and more fashion advertising. In 1984 Stavrinos visited Japan as a guest lecturer at the Tokyo Designer's College.

Contact: George Stavrinos, 76 West 86th Street, New York, New York 10024. Tel: (212) 724 1557.

STEVEN STIPELMAN

Steven Stipelman was born in New York in 1944. He studied art at the High School of Music and Art and then fashion at the Fashion Institute of Technology.

His first major job as an illustrator was at the specialty store Henri Bendel in New York, where he did all the fashion advertising for newspapers and catalogues. In 1965 he went to *Women's Wear Daily* and was sent to cover all the international collections – his sketches were wired to New York for instant publication. He would also cover gala parties and receptions, reporting on who was wearing what, where and when.

Today Stipelman is a successful freelance illustrator, and he still does advance fashion sketches for *Women's Wear Daily* of social luminaries such as Nancy Reagan and Princess Caroline of Monaco, often working only from descriptions of what they will be wearing at particular functions. Stipelman's other accounts include the cosmetic companies Estée Lauder, Charles of the Ritz, Orlane and Clairol; *Vogue* and Simplicity Patterns; the department stores Marshall Field and Lord & Taylor; textile companies such as

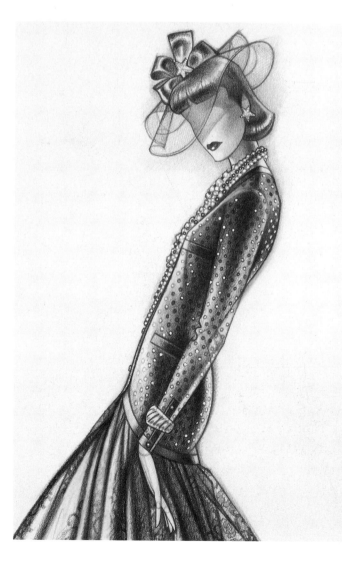

Left: Advertisement for Bergdorf Goodman, published in the 'New York Sunday Times', 1983. Graphite pencil drawing by George Stavrinos.
Above: Fashion forecast drawing by Steven Stipelman for 'Women's Wear Daily', 1985.

Celanese, Du Pont and American Silk Mills; and clothing companies Adèle Simpson, Hanes and Helga.

He is on the teaching faculty at Parsons School of Art, and lectures on fashion illustration at the Fashion Institute of Technology, Mount Mary College, Stephens College, the Art Institute of Philadelphia and others.

Contact: Steven Stipelman, 201 East 21st Street, New York, New York. Tel: (212) 260 6563.

HÉLÈNE TRAN

Hélène Tran was born in Paris in 1954. She studied illustration at the École Supérieure d'Art Graphique in Paris and has been a freelance illustrator since 1980.

She is a regular contributor to *Vogue* (both American and British), *GAP* (for whom she designs many covers) and *La Mode en Peinture*, and she has designed publicity material for clients who include the couture house of Jean Patou, the Printemps and Galeries Lafayette department stores and the shoe designer Roger Vivier.

Contact: Hélène Tran Kim, 6 villa Collet, 75014 Paris. Tel: 45 42 82 59.

Jewellery advertisement for Galeries Lafayette, 1986. Pastel drawing by Hélène Tran.

TONY VIRAMONTES

Tony Viramontes was born in 1960 in Los Angeles of Mexican parents, and he travelled extensively as a child. He studied fine art and photography in New York before switching to fashion and beauty illustration. This interest inevitably led him to Europe, where he lived in Venice and Paris, whose art traditions he finds inspiring.

Viramontes has worked for magazines and fashion houses in Italy, France and Japan, illustrating some inspired campaigns for Yves Saint Laurent, Claude Montana and Valentino.

He lists among his influences Man Ray, Jean Cocteau, Degas, Matisse, Egon Schiele, Picasso, Fellini and Tom of Finland. In 1984 an exhibition of his work was held in Paris.

Since 1984 Viramontes has been experimenting with 'photo-illustration' – drawing over photographs – and he plans to direct films.

Contact: Marion de Baupré, 26 rue des Plantes, 75014 Paris. Tel: 45 39 88 32.

Poster design for 'The Best Five Designers' celebration in Tokyo, Winter 1983, by Tony Viramontes.

ZOLTAN

Zoltan was born in Hungary in 1957. After finishing school in 1975 he worked for a fashion magazine in Budapest for three years, and also as a freelance photographer for theatres and exhibitions. In 1979 he left Hungary and was granted political asylum in Britain. He attended a fashion/business studies B.A. course at the American College in London, and in 1981 started working as a freelance illustrator. His portfolio of drawings of bizarre, dream-like figures, a Wagnerian or Fellini-esque pageant of eccentric and disturbing characters, took London's fashion editors by surprise and won Zoltan his first commission from *Vogue* in 1982, which was followed by regular pages and portraits.

In 1984 he visited New York – working for *The New York Times*, American *Vogue*, and *Interview* – and Paris, where he worked for *Libération* and on international press releases for the Fédération Française du Prêt-a-porter Féminin. He now divides his time between London, Paris and Tokyo, and his clients and commissions include: in Britain, *Harper's & Queen, Tatler, Cosmopolitan, Company, Honey* and *Working Woman*, advertising campaigns for Young & Rubican (AEG domestic appliances), Fabrex exhibitions and record sleeves; in Italy, *Lei* and *Donna*; in Japan, Issey Miyake, *Ryuko Tsushin*, Shiseido and Suntory.

Contact: Zoltan, Flat 5, King's Mansions, Lawrence Street, London SW3. Tel: (01) 351 6254. Telex: Z.I.P. 263 250 TELEX G. Fax: Z.I.P. 349 0049.

Unpublished image by Zoltan, 1986.